FINDING YOUR B.I.G.

(BIG IMPOSSIBLE GOAL)

FINDING YOUR B.I.G.

(BIG IMPOSSIBLE GOAL)

OLUBODE SHAWN BROWN

Cover design by Olubode Shawn Brown
Interior layout and design by www.writingnights.org
Book preparation by Chad Robertson
ISBN: 978-0-9903058-2-8

LIBRARY OF CONGRESS CATALOGING-IN-PUBLICATION DATA:
NAMES: Brown, Olubode Shawn. author
TITLE: Finding Your B.I.G. / Olubode Shawn Brown
DESCRIPTION: Banyan Tree Press, New York, 2021
IDENTIFIERS: ISBN 978-0-9903058-2-8 (Perfect bound) |
SUBJECTS: | Non-Fiction | Personal Growth |
CLASSIFICATION: Pending
LC record pending

Book Website:
www.bloomeducation.institute

Published by
Banyan Tree Press
445 W 125th Street
New York, NY 10027

Printed in the United States of America.
Printed on acid-free paper.

24 23 22 21 8 7 6 5 4 3 2 1

For the Family.

*"Nothing is impossible; the word itself says,
I'M POSSIBLE."*

—AUDREY HEPBURN

CONTENTS

WELCOME

Welcome to your **Finding Your B.I.G. Journey**. We are each Spiritual beings on a human journey bearing unique and valuable gifts to exchange with each other at a time when these gifts are *all* urgently needed.

My name is Olubode. I am author of **BLOOM, The Essential Journey** ~ *A New Guide to Balance, Growth & Wellbeing*. It is an honor to be on this journey with you.

Have you ever had those days when the path from here to there is not clear, or days when you seem to have lost track of why you are doing what you are doing?

Perhaps you too have felt that there is so much you want to do with all the skills and ideas you have but wondered how to bring them all into focus to have a real experience of play and adventure.

Surely we have all wondered, "How can I do what I truly love, make a living at it and make a difference in the world?"

Maybe like me, you have asked, "How do I attract and retain the right people to my team?"

These days we all seem to be asking, "How do I balance it all?"

With the global pandemic the need to answer these questions has become more urgent.

The 2020 pandemic has revealed what has been a long-lingering issue for many: the need to ***balance how we work and our wellbeing.***

- Why do we work?
- When do we work?
- Who do we work with, and for?
- What do we create?
- Where does it all lead?

These are the questions that now have our full attention.

Since 2020 there has been a significant increase in the numbers of people resigning their jobs, looking for new careers, starting new businesses, or simply just taking a break from life as usual.

According to **Anthony Klotz,** a professor of management at Texas A&M's Mays Business School, who has researched the psychology of quitting for much of his career, "We all want to pursue life, liberty and happiness, and many of us have realized our job isn't the best way to get there."

The BOOMER generation is ready to leave the workforce while many are still full of passion. Millennials and Generation Xers, who now make up the vast majority of the global workforce, are feeling more unsupported and disconnected from work activities they spend most of their waking hours doing.

Independent artists and entrepreneurs need to be careful so as not to duplicate the working styles we shunned and unwittingly create the same stressors for ourselves. Many of us are under-resourced and need the continuity of a committed team. All this, while dealing with an uncertain and rapidly changing global economy. We too are finding the need to pause to find a bigger "why" and re-imagine and re-align our lives with what really matters to us.

For me, the answers to these questions start with the **Finding Your B.I.G.** Journey. B.I.G. is an acronym for "Big

Impossible (or I'm Possible) Goal."

I believe we were all born with such a goal inside us. So whether you are an independent artist, employee or entrepreneur, you have one. If you are unconscious of it, it gives you repeated wake-up calls for you to follow what the philosopher Joseph Campbell called "your bliss."

On this journey a B.I.G. is a self-energizing, measurable goal that is aligned with your vision, pain, passion, talents, and gifts. Not every big goal is a B.I.G. A goal becomes B.I.G. when it is aligned with your vision, pain, passion, talents, and gifts. A B.I.G. symbolizes a desired result and a process, connected to your deep story.

In this book we will journey together to fine-tune this alignment.

The more aware you are of your B.I.G., the more you are able to co-create your life in cooperation with it.

To the extent that your work is designed with your B.I.G. in mind, you will do your best work, be less stressed, and feel more connected, more relevant and purposeful.

The purpose of this book is to help you to bring your B.I.G. to more conscious awareness. Its intention is to provide you with a new tool in the form of five questions with which to unfold for yourself a life of greater satisfaction, purpose and fulfilment.

In 2017, I published **BLOOM, The Essential Journey,** ***A New Guide to Balance, Growth & Wellbeing***. In this book I addressed the impossibility of the equation we have been presented with: LIFE on the one hand, and WORK on the other. In it, readers were introduced to a new equation, one that uses the five elements of creation as metaphors to reveal another way of finding balance in our lives.

Today in the wake of the global pandemic in which the artificial divide between life and work has been fully exposed, we are experiencing unprecedented levels of burnout, loss of energy, lack of focus and a pent-up demand for change.

Many have taken this time to pause, to slow down and reflect. We have found the importance of pursuing creative passions, of learning something new, or reading a book. We are re-examining the life balance choices we have made.

For many it has been a process of trial and error. For example, some have started businesses simply because it was a good idea at the time, and the demand was there, or the product was promising. We did so without the passion or the compassion it takes to really create value for others and a healing journey for ourselves.

Others of us remain in unsatisfying jobs, afraid and not knowing how to take the leap without losing our financial safety net.

Depression, anxiety and stress are common problems for

modern workers. Gallup's 2012 worldwide poll concluded 13% of employees are engaged at work; 63% are not engaged, sleepwalking through their day. Twenty-four percent are actively disengaged—pretending to work, but really being counter-productive. Many of us deaden ourselves to get through the work day. We are engaged with work that does not challenge us or cause us to change and grow in a healthy way or make a difference in the lives of others. Solutions are clear; it is widely understood that we must repurpose our working environment for greater fulfillment and productivity.

And then there are working creatives, who value real creative freedom and want to monetize their work for their survival, but fear the loss of that freedom and the sanctuary their work provides.

The purpose of this book is to help us to re-align with our deeper purpose and unique niche without unnecessary trial and error by engaging with five simple yet powerful questions.

Why?

Because it has been my experience that when these questions are asked and answered deeply and regularly, they align a powerful self-energizing channel within us. This channel, when aligned, provides the foundation that allows us to:

- Know our next steps in each moment, clearly
- Work with a sense of curiosity, play and adventure
- Be visible and powerfully negotiate our real value

- Attract the right people to our teams
- Find a new, more fluid center from which to discover in each moment the balance we need.

Perhaps you are as confused as I was by the competing ideas about the meaning of words like "purpose," "passion," "gifts," "vision," "mission," "goals," and "talent." Too often these words are used to provide guidance without an understanding of this elemental sequenced channel out of which our lives are unfolding.

With this misunderstanding we are left asking questions like: *Do I need to pursue my passion or just go with the flow? What if I don't know my purpose? Will it find me? What if I can't see my vision—does that mean I will perish? What if I don't know my gifts or know what I am passionate about? What's the difference between a gift and a talent?*

I believe **FINDING YOUR B.I.G.** is needed now to put this confusion to rest.

Indeed, passion alone is not enough—neither is talent or a gift, for that matter—and a vision without a goal-oriented action cannot be fully born. Yet these ideas, when understood together and sequenced elementally, provide a unique roadmap for each individual life.

I promise you that after you have taken this journey and completed its exercises, you will never again be in any doubt about your life's purpose. Words like passion, talent, gift, mission or vision will no longer confuse. What's more, you will have found your B.I.G.—one that will grow and manifest over time with your care and attention to it. Once you have found it, you will be able to find other B.I.G. people. In this way, we will be able to work together toward a collective good.

But first we have to be willing to pause.

I remember placing my business on pause about 15 years ago. I was at a crossroads. I was working as a lawyer and corporate consultant at the time. I loved photography and I was good at it, so I turned to doing that professionally. I also threw parties from time to time. I was also leading workshops and seminars. Frankly, I was all over the place and I knew it.

I really could not go on. I was pulled by passions and talents that I had, but not quite sure how to put it all together. I was not sure what to do next. I would start one thing and then stop, then start another. So my income stopped and started too. Eventually I lost passion for what I was doing, as well as the confidence of the people who supported me. I had felt a change coming, and I too was changing, but I was not quite sure what it was or how to respond.

I was at the end of a cycle of doing things one way. I could feel myself losing my way. So I took a break from New York City and went to North Carolina to get it together. Sometimes we have to do that to really get a handle on where we are and where we want to go.

Right now, this may be a good time for you to pause, reinvent, and re-imagine.

I was very blessed to be able to take the timeout to pause. My friend Orin invited me to North Carolina. I hung out there with him for months. Each morning I sat with him and he gently helped me to remember my own story.

When we are on the run we don't give ourselves the time to reflect. I know how that is. I had the privilege to pause, to slow down and think. My need was urgent. I was blessed with a great listener.

I stopped and took time to reflect and began to ask myself powerful questions.

Orin knew me well. He is a friend who knew my history. With a few simple questions he re-directed me to a new path that led to the creation of **BLOOM** and its brands—**The BLOOM Live Free**, the **BLOOM Festival**, and to writing ***BLOOM: The Essential Journey***. In time I also founded **BLOOM Education**, and built a beautiful community of "BLOOMERS" from all over the world.

THE ELEMENTS OF THIS JOURNEY

Finding Your B.I.G. Journey is made up of five steps. At each step I will guide you as you find your answers to five questions. These are five elementally calibrated questions designed to tap into five elemental forces that nurture and grow your life and all life.

All growing things need vital life nutrients. These are the things that help us human beings to bloom.

In my first book **BLOOM: The Essential Journey** - ***A New Guide to Balance, Growth & Wellbeing***, I provided the rationale for the use of the five elements of creation as metaphors to help grow and balance our lives. For a more complete understanding of this, please read ***Chapter II -- The New Life Balance.***

I am forever grateful to the wisdom of my African ancestors and the teaching of Malidoma Some, an elder of the Dagara people of Burkina Faso, who brought his knowledge of an indigenous African elemental worldview into clear focus for me. It is this wisdom that most inspires me. In my work, among other things, I use these elements to help us understand the five essential life-nutrients that we all need as human beings.

The five questions at each step of the journey connect us with our own power—the five elements of creation within us.

Here are the five elements and the questions asked at each of the five steps of this Finding Your B.I.G. Journey.

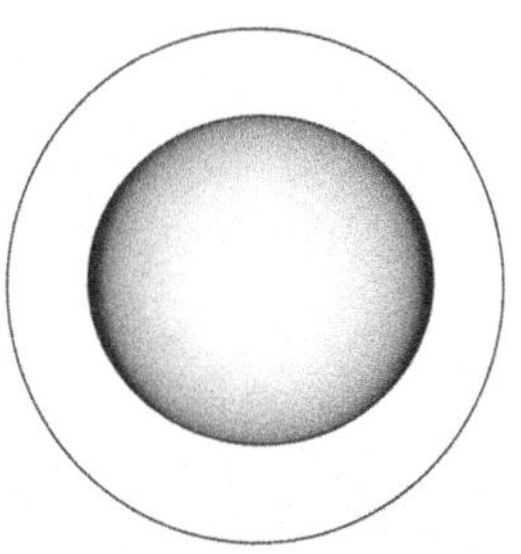

MINERAL

— the energy that allows you to hear your own voice.

MINERAL QUESTION~ WHAT IS MY VISION?

NATURE

— the energy that allows you to move and change effortlessly

NATURE QUESTION ~ WHAT ARE MY PASSIONS?

FIRE

— the energy that allows you to see yourself clearly

FIRE QUESTION ~ WHAT ARE MY TALENTS?

WATER

— the energy that allows you to
connect deeply with others

WATER QUESTION ~ WHAT IS MY HEALING GIFT?

EARTH
—the balancing energy helps us to navigate
and be safe in our world.
EARTH QUESTION ~ WHAT IS MY BIG IMPOSSIBLE GOAL?

QUESTIONS THAT MATTER

Each of five questions of this Finding Your B.I.G. Journey is also a reflection of the five fundamental existential questions of our human journey.

Right now you may be asking:

- How do I know whether this move or that move is right for me?
- How do I do this in the present climate with its environment of uncertainty?
- How do I get people to work together peacefully?
- How do I do this and make sure that I can take care of my family?
- How do I balance it all and make sure that I take care of my health?

These "how to..." questions can rob us of our Soul's magic. "How to..." questions are often driven by our fear of not being enough and not having enough. Essentially, we ask "how-to" questions to get what we desire from the world around us. Because our desires are also needs that have become wants, we ask for them most urgently, if not desperately, of others.

When we do this others are always there to give us those answers. Yet somehow they are not satisfying, because they are always someone else's answer, not our own.

Here is a new set of questions to help you remember your story and find the answers that are right for you. These new questions will help you to tap into our own individual and collective power. The more deeply you ask them, they will lead you naturally, and seemingly magically, to *"how to..."* in each moment as needed.

Here are the five questions. At BLOOM we call them the 5Ws.

1. WHY DO I EXIST?

What is my story? Why have I had the journey, trauma, experiences I have had? This gives rise to the MINERAL question: What is my VISION? MINERAL is the element that holds your memories, your stories and your voice. It holds the memory of the VISION we carry in our bones.

2. WHEN DO I COME ALIVE?

This is the NATURE question. NATURE is the element that inspires change. It is the element that brings things alive and keeps things moving along. This gives rise to the NATURE question: What are my PASSIONS?

WHO AM I?

Who am I that is valuable? What am I being paid for, complimented on, or acknowledged for by others? This inspires the FIRE question: What are my TALENTS? FIRE is the element that gives us visibility and value in the world.

WHAT IS MY ROLE IN THE WORLD?

What is my healing role in the world?
WATER is the element of peace and reconciliation. It helps us connect deeply to each other. This inspires the WATER question: What is my GIFT?

WHERE AM I & WHERE AM I GOING?

Where am I, and where am I going? This inspires the EARTH question: What is my BIG IMPOSSIBLE GOAL? EARTH is the element that gives us our sense of balance and perspective.

These are questions that only you can choose to answer for yourself.

Each of us is asking and answering these questions throughout our lifetimes. The answers we get constitute our unique journey.

At the root of these five questions are the five fundamental desires we ALL have. We ask questions to find these five life-giving nutrients that ultimately we find within ourselves.

These life-nutrients are:

— MINERAL: The DESIRE TO HEAR our own story and be heard
— NATURE: THE DESIRE TO EXPERIENCE CHANGE, and not feel stuck
— FIRE: THE DESIRE TO REALLY SEEN & VALUED
— WATER: THE DESIRE TO FEEL CONNECTED
— EARTH: THE DESIRE TO BELONG and feel at HOME

As we ask these questions more deeply we begin to:

- Re-connect to and heal the wounded child in us.
- Dream again
- Recover hope—a sense of play, possibility and wonder returns to our lives
- See ourselves and our value more
- Find connections to other dreamers
- Expand our ability to innovate collectively with others who are asking and finding in themselves answers to the same questions.

When all the questions of this Journey are answered

sequentially, a powerful picture of your life's purpose and possibilities will begin to emerge.

A WORD ABOUT WORKING TOGETHER

The ultimate goal of this process is to create a global platform for us all to be able to work together collectively. The Finding Your B.I.G. Journey is the first step, inasmuch as it provides a shared language with which to engage each other.

By taking this journey you are stepping into a new kind of collective power, where sharing your deep story among fellow collective leaders can create the strong bonds with which you can do the impossible. It is our shared stories that allow us to solve the dilemma of balancing the individual self interest and the collective good.

I recommend that before you do anything else collectively, in a team or group, that you pause and ask and answer the questions of this journey for yourself, and listen to others in your circle as they share their answers to these questions.

In this way we will be able to:

- **Hear** our collective vision and the ways in which each person holds a piece of that vision.
- **Experience** ourselves as part of a shared, self-generated enterprise of collective leaders, each taking the circle on a powerful adventure.

- **Appreciate** the value and leverage of the individual resources that the collective has within it and know that these resources are enough.
- **Connect** with others and be responsible for our own emotions, so that we can lead with greater empathy in our dealings with each other.
- **Serve** the collective good by making the individual's wellbeing our first priority

At BLOOM this is what we are learning and practicing in order to better create an environment of real equity, one that allows us to work together sustainably and profitably.

This is what's possible, and it starts with Finding Your B.I.G.

HOW TO TAKE THIS JOURNEY

Each word in the questions of this journey is used with intention. The instructions offered are intended to deepen and expand the meaning of each word and place it within an energetic order in which it can be more easily understood. So when reading, suspend for a moment the meaning and associations you may have brought to these words: VISION, PASSION, TALENT, GIFT, and GOAL.

Do your best to answer each question completely before moving on to the next.

If you need to, pause and reflect before moving on.

When you have completed each step you can go back and refine your answers. Over time your answers will deepen and prove to be an important compass as your life unfolds.

In my experience, taking this journey fully is among one of the most courageous things one can do. I never fail to be inspired and deeply moved by those who do, and who share their story.

If possible, take this journey with a trusted friend or one of our BLOOM Certified guides—someone who can hold you gently as you move through each step.

If you can, view the **Finding Your B.I.G. Online Master Class** as you go. In this Master Class, you will see me walking through each of the five steps of this journey with Shannon Shird, an amazing, creative Entrepreneur and visionary.

However you choose to journey...

This is Our Time to BLOOM.

Olubode
October 5th, 2021
Harlem, New York

THE FINDING YOUR B.I.G JOURNEY

"Where there is no vision,
the people perish..."
~ PROVERBS 29:18

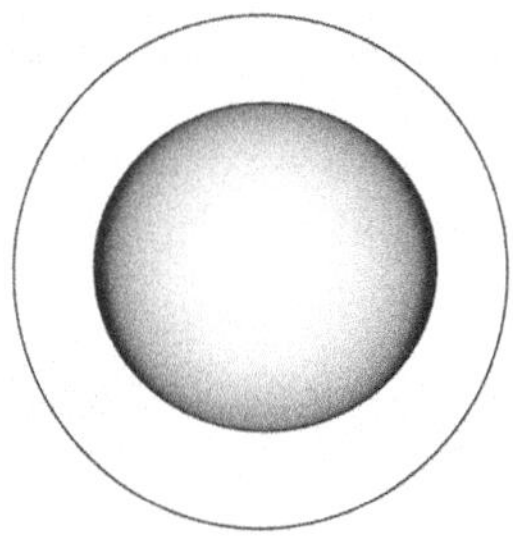

STEP I
WHAT IS MY VISION?

Chances are you know this quote from the King James version of the Bible. I have often wondered, *What is the vision that Solomon refers to?*

On this journey a vision is first heard and then seen, but with inner eyes. I invite you to think of a vision as a memory of the world you came from. It is the world that you saw before you had what we call "your complaint."

Identifying your complaint and then turning around to see

a vision of your world, the world you carry in your bones for everyone, is the first step of this journey.

Your vision shows up most brightly in the dark moment just before your light was first dimmed, and it continues to show up each time throughout our lives when our lights go dim.

Unearthing your vision means reading the hidden clues in your complaints.

WHAT IS A COMPLAINT?

A complaint is an authentic expression of the wounds we have experienced in our lifetime. **The deepest ones first surface when we are children, before the age of seven.** The complaint is usually triggered by something that happened early in life. So to find it, begin to think of an incident that happened very early in your life that interrupted your world. That interruption triggered powerful emotions. We made decisions about who we are and the nature of life and what we would be in order to get the love we need. What happened and the resulting series of decisions is what's called your complaint.

My complaint can be summarized as: "They can't see me; I will show them."

For me it arose from an experience of aloneness and disconnection triggered by well-meaning people who were charged with my care.

There I stood, embarrassed, in front of children in a classroom at the age of six. I remember hearing their laughter and losing sight of myself, as if I were swallowed up in darkness. "I will show them," was the form my complaint took. In my mind I was clear that this was not right.

As I have grown older there have been other times when that shadow has come over me.

These days, anything that reminds me of this sequence of events triggers my fear of invisibility and betrayal. Each time I choose to run to the front of the room and stand for something, that fear and complaint is there. "They don't see me, and when they do, I will mess up and they will turn on me."

For many our complaint comes from feeling that we do not belong in the family, community, or country in which we grew up. For others, it is a complaint triggered by experiences that made us feel smaller because our voice was not heard. There are also complaints triggered by a need to escape, change, and take control of things in order to survive. Though we can all find times when we had all of these experiences and complaints, there are one or two of the same complaints that persist—that repeat themselves over time.

What is the fundamental complaint that you have had about life?

Fixing that thing drives you. When triggered you can feel the sting of what happened.

Whatever it was that happened gave voice to your first complaint.

Identifying our complaint with fierce compassion is the first step in voicing your vision and finding your purpose.

On this journey we say that your purpose is to be an ambassador—a representative of the world of your vision.

One of my teachers, **Rev. Michael Beckwith**, often talks about being "pulled by a vision." In this analogy, imagine yourself being pulled through a field joyously by an invisible force. Imagine that soon you run smack into a tree. What would be the first thing you say?

"________?________"

That's your complaint as you wake up to your human experience.

This is what happens to us as children. We are happily being pulled along, then we run into life's experiences.

Our complaints are our first attempts to articulate the vision that we each carry, and they keep pulling it forward.

When you had your first complaint, it distorted things; it created a hole in the magnetic pull of your natural vision that we felt without words when we were born. This tear becomes a lens through which the physical world appears, but shaped by contours of the distortion caused by the hole.

Your complaint tells you what your vision is not. If we can access what it is not, then we can begin to imagine in language the feel of the vision we carry.

In doing this work, I have seen that the deepest wounds first surface when we are children before the age of seven. Our complaint has its roots there.

We are better able to help others when we have a compassionate engagement with our own pain and its healing.

THE FIVE EMOTIONAL WOUNDS & COMPLAINTS

Here are the five basic complaints we have as human beings.

1. [MINERAL] I AM NOT HEARD. I was silenced. I could not say anything. Whatever I said was ignored. Nothing I say will ever make a difference. I have not been heard.
2. [NATURE] THIS IS HOPELESS. I AM STUCK. I was held down/back. I did not have a clue what was happening. I was no longer in control. Things were out of control. I am not being allowed to change.
3. [FIRE] I AM NOT SEEN. I FELT INVISIBLE. People saw things in me that were not true. I felt like I had no value. I could not see myself. Nothing I did was good enough. Something was wrong with me.
4. [WATER] I AM ABANDONED. I was left alone. I was

alone with my feelings. I showed how I felt and I was betrayed.

5. [EARTH] I AM VULNERABLE & UNSAFE. I was not able to make sense of things. I did not have a compass. I felt lost. The order of things was broken. There was not enough. Things were chaotic. I am vulnerable, physical and emotionally.

We all say these complaints or some version of them. Our complaints are what we have been working at healing all our lives.

Often we have followed and developed our passions and talents in order to fix them.

From time to time, I hear someone say, "I don't have a complaint about my life."

If this is you, here is what I would offer: Gently, look more closely. Shame, guilt and anger often stop us from acknowledging our complaints. This stops us from getting the healing we need.

Your complaint is simply information about what you are here to heal for yourself and others.

Admitting your complaint does not mean you are still a victim, or in reaction to it. When you recognize the underlying trauma that caused it, you step into owning your own healing and the medicine for others just like you.

In this way you begin to break the cycle of hurt, where "hurt people hurt people."

In this first step of the journey we will stop and turn from that complaint to see your life's vision. Doing this can transform your anger and rage into a powerful intention.

I have found that being aware of our pain and our journey to heal have three phases.

In the first phase it is like a fish in cloudy water and you can't see it except for intermittent glimpses.

Then there is the phase when we can see it, and we identify our emotional pain as who we are. Here we are, our pain. Here we say things like "I am angry."

In the third phase we can feel our pain, yet work with it creatively—healing while using it to serve others who, like ourselves, are on their own healing journey.

We are all at different places on our journey.

Are you at the point in your life when the memory of pain can be creatively engaged?

Ask yourself this:

If you were to identify one complaint that you would say has been the theme for your life, what would it be? Your complaint has a sound. It's something you have said repeatedly to yourself, and acted upon.

HERE ARE THE MAIN THEMES OF FIVE COMPLAINTS

MINERAL
"I have not been heard."
This gives rise to the pain of feeling irrelevant.

NATURE
"I am not allowed to change" or "This will never change."
This gives rise to the pain of hopelessness.

FIRE
"I am not seen and valued."
This gives rise to the pain of being invisible or discounted.

WATER
"I am abandoned/betrayed."
This gives rise to the pain of loneliness.

EARTH
"I am not safe here."
This gives rise to the pain of feeling homeless and disconnected.

DO THE FOLLOWING TASKS TO IDENTIFY YOUR COMPLAINT:

Do these tasks now.

TASK A ~ RECALL

This is a drawing exercise. Being good at drawing is not required. First turn to a clean page in your journal and draw whatever represents a timeline of your life, from the time you were born to the age you are now. It could be a straight line up or down the page, or it could be spirals or shapes, representing various decades.

Along that timeline, begin to recall first the times in your life when you light shone brightest. These are the moments when you can recall yourself perhaps with the greatest sense of ease, freedom and belonging. Or perhaps it was a time when you felt most connected to a place or person. On your timeline create an image or symbol that represents what happened.

Next recall the times in your life when your light was dimmed. These were the times when the future looked bleak—times when you might have experienced being disconnected from life and the people around you. On your timeline create an image or symbol that represents what happened.

When was your light *first* dimmed? When did you first experience a sense of disconnection? Often this happens when you are silenced, separated from others in some way or left feeling different. Note we are not trying to fix things, just to identify it as best we can and as deeply as we can at this time. In a journal or in the lines provided below recall happened. What were the facts, as you experienced them?

HERE IS WHAT HAPPENED....

____

____

____

____

____

TASK B ~ IDENTIFY THE FEELING

What did you feel? Note which of the following most closely reflects what you felt at the time.

I felt I was ....

- Not heard and silenced
- Stuck or no longer in control
- Not seen and valued
- Abandoned or felt betrayed
- Physically and emotionally unsafe.

In your own words, describe how this experience made you feel.

HERE IS HOW THIS EXPERIENCE MADE ME FEEL...

____

____

____

____

____

TASK C ~ YOUR DECISION ABOUT YOURSELF

When your light was first dimmed, what decision did you make about yourself?

Which phrases from the list below most closely resonate?
I am not heard.
I am stuck and no longer in control.
I am invisible, not seen.
I am abandoned and alone.
I am not safe.

How would you say them in your own words?

I DECIDED THAT I AM....

____

____

TASK D ~ YOUR DECISION ABOUT LIFE

What decision did you make about the world and/or others?

Which of the following most resonates most for you?

I will not be listened to.
Life is out of my control.
They will not see me.
People will leave.
The world is unsafe.

How would you express the decision you made about life in your own words?

I DECIDED THAT....

____

____

____

TASK E ~ REFLECT ON HOW YOU DECIDED TO COPE

Given what happened, what would you say was the decision you most likely made about how to be, in order to get the love you needed?

Don't sugar-coat it. Try to say it as only you can.

I DECIDED THAT I WOULD BE....

____

____

____

Please take a moment now, if needed, to pause and, if needed, move around a bit. Take the time to reflect on your answers before moving on.

NOTES ON VISION

Your vision for the world is revealed by the earliest complaints you had about your life. Our earliest complaint follows us throughout our lives. Our complaints come out of early traumas of being told how to be, being silenced, or feeling stuck, abandoned or unsafe. Yet behind your complaint is a POWERFUL VISION of a world in which this complaint and the trauma that caused it could not exist!

As we wake up to our human journey, among our first words are a complaint. Before then, as small children we seem to have a pure vision of the world that we simply sense. Then it happens. Something happens that does not feel like that world, and our first complaint is voiced. Over time this complaint is reinforced by our experiences, and these experiences begin to dim our vision.

Our voice first wakes up as a complaint. Embedded in the things we complain about is your vision—the vision of the world you saw before it happened. On the other side of your complaint is vision. If you turn your complaint around, you clearly see the vision of the world you came with. It is the world we are each here to remember and to unfold.

Can you see the kind of world you want to be living in—one in which your complaint could not exist? Can you describe that world?

In the next task you will be asked to give voice to your vision. I recommend that you begin with these words:

"I can see a world where..."

End with the words:

.... for everyone."

When we make our vision not just for ourselves and people like us, it holds more energy. Our vision, when articulated in this way and not as a complaint, begins the process of its manifestation and our healing.

Imagine the world you come from

WHAT KIND OF WORLD CAN YOU SEE IN WHICH YOUR COMPLAINT COULD NOT HAVE BEEN MADE BY ANYONE?

Can you imagine a world where that complaint could never arise?

- What did the world feel like before you had your first complaint?
- What were some of the qualities of that world?
- Write those qualities down.

____

____

____

TASK G ~ GIVE VOICE TO YOUR VISION

Write your vision statement out in this form:

"I can see a world where ... for everyone!"

MY VISION IS....

I CAN SEE A WORLD WHERE ....

___

___

___

Here is my vision:

"A world of love, where every gift is delivered, every journey is celebrated and all are free."

Now that you have voiced your vision, I invite you to live from this moment on as a representative of the world of your vision. What I have discovered is that our vision is the source of our lives. Keeping it sacred, fresh, vital, gives it potency. A vision is seen with inner eyes, yet gives us new eyes as we carry it into the world, with compassion, with the sense that there is enough, and with the awareness that it is becoming real. To carry your vision into the world is one of the most courageous things we can do.

A vision is what gives us new life!

"Anything... that does not bring you alive
is too small for you."

~ DAVID WHYTE, *THE HOUSE OF BELONGING*

STEP II
WHAT ARE YOUR PASSIONS?

What is called your passions are the actions associated with the element we call nature. This element, though seasonal, is also spontaneous and unpredictable, full of genius. These are the activities to which we are drawn and naturally committed.

Our passions reveal our underlying motivations and commitments. We can do them endlessly, it seems at times. We don't have to struggle to do them, and somehow even in the midst of uncertainty, we find a space to do them.

Your B.I.G. has room in it for ALL your passions. This is what you do to give yourself that feeling of being alive—the things that take you into an unbounded field of play. It is the way that you and only you can move in the world. Passions have their own order and sense of natural discipline. We don't have to go after them. It would seem we come pre-loaded with them in us.

In this step of the journey we ask: What are your passions? What are the things that bring you alive?

Whatever they are, write them ALL down, even the ones you might have started and stopped. Leave none out.

Sometimes we are ashamed of our passions, or embarrassed by them. Admit them. Let them in, as long as they do not harm you or anyone. It is what you naturally/spontaneously can do endlessly. You don't have to be good at it, yet it is how you practice your unique style, and it sets you free.

Our passions are important because they reveal our natural style/our personal style, and they will inform how we go after our B.I.G.

ELEMENTS OF PASSION

1. It is spontaneous
2. It's out of the box and you can do it endlessly, without regard for time. You can get lost doing it. You don't

have to discipline yourself in order to do it.

3. It reveals your genius.
4. It is effortless.
5. It's done in your unique style—there is no harm to anyone.

MY PASSIONS ARE...

____

____

____

____

____

"Your talent is God's gift to you. What you do with it is your gift back to God."

~ LEO BUSCAGLIA

STEP III WHAT ARE YOUR TALENTS?

So far we have worked through the MINERAL phase of the channel to find our voice. The element of mineral is a metaphor for VOICE. We have taken the voicing of your complaint and turned it around to begin to begin to put into words the vision of the land you come from—the land you are here to represent.

Next we move farther down the channel to the NATURE aspect of the channel. NATURE is used here as a metaphor for CHANGE: specifically in this context the things that "move" us, our PASSIONS.

Now we have come to the FIRE in the channel.

Fire is the element that is a metaphor for VISIBILITY & VALUE.

Here we are looking for the things that we are seen and valued for—our talents.

In this process of Finding Your B.I.G, the word "talent" has a specific meaning.

Our talents are the things that we do that others value in us.

Often they are what we have been paid to do. Sometimes they are the things we are simply acknowledged for, praised for or complimented for. Whether we are paid or complimented, our action is received and shines a light in someone's world. Your talent pulls other people around you to have that experience of your talent.

Our talents provide others with new information that is helpful and insightful.

Remember, your talent is distinct from your passion. You may have a talent that you are not passionate about, and you may have a passion that is also a talent. Not all talents are passions.

What are your talents?

List them all—the things that you are complimented for, that create an experience for others, that bring new knowledge, that bring you and the people around you new connections, and that you are paid in cash or a material exchange to provide.

Here is an instructive exchange that happened recently between me and a member of this journey, who I will call "Jose." It happened after attending a reading from his new book of poetry.

Jose:
"I just wanted to say a massive thank you for being there last night... It definitely was a bold move and I'm so glad I did it! I realized afterwards that it was a bit like a rite of passage - like I now feel genuinely like I've moved into that part of my identity called 'poet' and everybody there willed me along. I've come with a lot of gratitude and I know you've played a big part in just growing that faith. So thank you very much!"

Me:
"I had an amazing and insightful time. Though I must say that the fact that you were a poet, to my recollection, was not included in your Finding Your B.I.G. process. So I was a tad bit surprised at this beautiful body of work. Perhaps I am mistaken?"

Jose:
"Well, no, it wasn't included in finding my B.I.G. because I

still can't quite work out how everything fits together. I still think in terms of financial survival and from bad experiences in the past, I'm shying away from monetizing those passions that give me real freedom. So while I'd like to be able to integrate writing more, I'm still figuring out its place."

Me:
"Ahhhh, so perhaps here is an opportunity to put it in and see how your B.I.G Journey expands. The thing with a B.I.G. is that it does not require you not to know 'how." We often just get what we need at the moment to take the next step."

Begin to notice where you are leaving behind parts of yourself, whether it be a passion or a talent, because of the ways in which you now hold them or because of past experiences. As a creator you can choose to engage your creative journey as a service to humanity. Yet you must also keep your journey sacred and uniquely yours.

MY TALENTS ARE....

____

____

____

____

____

"What you are is God's gift to you, what you become is your gift to God."

~ HANS URS VON BALTHASAR, PRAYER

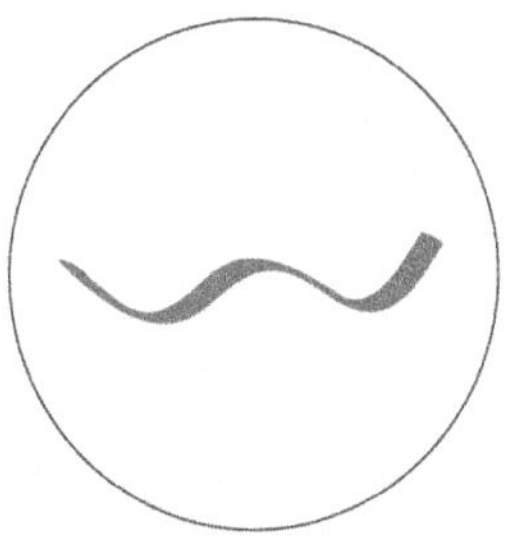

STEP IV
WHAT IS YOUR GIFT?

On this journey the word "gift" has a specific meaning. Your "gift" is the healing gift you make with your combined passions and talents. It is a gift you choose to create with the intention to heal the people who are now moving through the pain that gave rise to your complaint.

So here your gift is not something you are given; it is something you create for yourself and others.

Right now there is someone just like you who needs your

gift, even as they continue their own journey to unfolding their passions and talents. They need what you have learned so far.

This next step is a two-parter. There are two questions to be answered.

First...
Who are the people around you right now who can hear your story as their own?

Your story is your journey. It is how you rose beyond your complaint to be the person you are today, to enjoy the experiences you have had as you bring to life the world of your vision.

On this journey we recognize that the passions and talents you have, and how you have used them, have been the medicine you have been using to heal your own pain.

It seems we only get to keep what we give away.

The second question is...

What gift can you create with ALL your passions as talents to heal the pain of others who feel as you do?

Your gift can be in service to a community, a family, an enterprise, a movement, or individuals, to heal the pain of silencing, the sting of limiting words. Perhaps it is a gift that will give us a greater understanding of each other, or something that will give new meaning to our lives.

Your gift can be a product or a service. It can be virtual or digital. What is that vehicle for you? You may notice that you have several vehicles in mind. Consolidate them if you can into one vehicle—product or service. Make it the biggest package you can imagine.

As you answer this question, take a moment and recall your own pain and use it creatively. I have discovered that it is best to first identify your "market" and their "needs" through the experience of compassion.

Who feels right now what you feel? How will you help them journey? What gift will you give them?

What are the problems and challenges they are facing and what solutions do you have?

Remember to combine as many if not all, of your passions and talents as possible into the biggest package you can imagine. It can be in any form: a book, a group, a shop, a play, a movement, an organization, a business, a platform. Also remember you don't have to know how to do it at this moment. Once you have created your gift, you have provided a vehicle out of which the knowledge and skills can be developed, practiced and take shape.

What's necessary is that you be true to what you feel is

possible, to what connects you to people who can relate to you and who you can relate to, in a form that has the capacity to reach as many as possible.

MY HEALING GIFT IS....

____

____

____

____

____

THE ANATOMY OF B.I.G.

Before taking the final step on this journey, let's pause for a moment to take a closer look at the at the potential of having a Big Impossible Goal.

Have you ever worn a pair of shoes that were too small for your feet?

Someone may have given them to you, or you may have purchased them for yourself. Perhaps like me, you tried them on. At first, they looked good and felt comfortable, until you started to walk around in them for a while.

They hurt my feet.

Your B.I.G. is a goal that is the perfect fit for who you truly are.

It is a container for all your unique passions and talents. It is a tangible goal that can expand over time to hold more and more of everything you encounter and are experiencing in your life. Going after it will take you on the most thrilling adventure of your life because it will inspire your complete authenticity because it contains everything you desire and that which you most fear. Yet it holds the key to the experience of your true value. Pursuing it will heal your life and the lives of people who feel like you do. The best part is, once you find it and nurture it, it fulfills itself!

Pursuing anything else will feel like wearing shoes that are too small for your feet.

This Finding your B.I.G. Journey is the process by which you take ownership of your story and powerfully declare it. The power with which our stories are told is what allows us to experience the fulfillment and prosperity that's truly ours.

In working together collectively, it is necessary that we sit together to remember the most truthful and powerful stories we can tell about our lives. Your story and the stories of each person you meet are entangled—they intersect and connect. When we share them with each other, we are delivering gifts and messages to each other that are vital for our evolution, revolution and transformation of our shared world.

Your Big Impossible Goal completes your story. It sets your direction in terms that you and others can understand. It is not necessary that you or others even believe it. And what's more, you do not need to know how to do it.

What matters is that you feel its alignment to the vision you carry for the world—that you feel it provides a place for the authentic expression of your soul's journey.

Your B.I.G. is a symbolic representation of your VISION. It reminds you of the land you come from.

Think of Muhammad Ali, as the young boxer Cassius Clay, declaring at 22 years old that he was "the greatest boxer of all time," and you will get a sense of the power of a B.I.G.

The impossible is a dare.

So imagine that you are in the gym with your trainer, coach or training partner. It's time to step up, because you have been doing the same thing over and over and you have become bored and uninspired. Today your coach decides to increase the weight you have been lifting by 60% to challenge you. You see this and "Hell no!!!" escapes your lips. He smiles and takes off the weight and instead increases it by 20%. You look at this new challenge with a mixture of two emotions. On the one hand, you feel a tinge of fear, and right beside that is a feeling of excitement. It excites and scares you. Yet you breathe, straighten up and go for it.

When you set a goal that triggers this energy of excitement and fear, in your body we say you have found your B.I.G., except instead of weight, it is packed with all your passions and talents, the biggest vision for the world and for your own life and wellbeing.

A B.I.G. is the most powerful goal you can set.

Here are the five features that define a B.I.G.

1. It can hold everything & will get BIGGER.

You B.I.G. is the "why" of our human journey. Everything that happens to us presents a road map to its discovery and expansion. It is hidden behind the complaints we have about our lives and the current painful circumstances we find ourselves in, the shaming we may have experienced as small children, our experiences of disconnection from others and the feeling that no place is safe. It holds the things we can play at endlessly that reveal our unique genius. It holds the things that we are valued for and counted on to do. Your B.I.G. is the reason you are born, and it gets bigger and more powerful the more of yourself you pour into it. It will engage you completely.

2. It is a thrilling journey.

A thrill is that feeling you get when you are afraid yet excited at the same time.

This is the feeling you get when you have found your B.I.G. Pursuing it will take you on a path bordered by your desires on the one hand and your fears on the other.

At every step you will be entering new territory. You will lose your balance and find it again and again, until you develop your own weird way of walking through the middle ground. Walking this thrilling path will change you profoundly as you step forward in your own unique, unbounded style.

3. It's valuable and rewarding.

Pursuing your B.I.G. will mean that you will be more visible as you take a stand for your own value and the gift that you are here to deliver. The more clearly you stand for your own value, the more you will be able to see and stand for the value of others.

The more powerful your stand for your value, the more you and the people around you will be valued for what you do. The more authentic your stand, the greater the value you will receive and increase in the way of acknowledgement, new and insightful experiences, new knowledge, people connections and material support.

4. You Cannot Do It Alone

A true B.I.G. is something you cannot accomplish by yourself. No one accomplishes anything that is truly meaningful and lasting alone. A B.I.G. requires a collective of people who have shared visions, who can playfully create together, support each other emotionally and feast together on shared resources. Your B.I.G. will help you find your tribe.

5. It's big, impossible & yet specific

It is BIG because you have never engaged in this goal before. It is IMPOSSIBLE because it comes from a vision of the world for which there is no physical evidence—nothing in your known world suggests that it will ever be possible. A B.I.G. exists in a space outside your known world. It is a goal that you do not know how to do. Yet it is a GOAL because it is specific and measurable. In other words, you will know when it's been achieved.

"Impossible is a dare... Impossible is nothing."

~ MUHAMMAD ALI

STEP V
WHAT IS YOUR BIG IMPOSSIBLE GOAL?

This is where I must caution you and reassure you. It is at this step that we often stop. Suddenly our minds get fuzzy, and we struggle to state a goal that is measurable and specific. To find your B.I.G. we must connect your complaint and the vision you carry for the world, and the passions and talents you have used to be here now.

Here are some of the things that may be going through your mind:

"What if I set this goal, say I am going to do it and don't do it—then I would not have kept my word." I will respond here to this. There is a difference between *keeping* your word and *being* your word. The goals we set and the promises we make have intention behind them. In the process of asking and answering the four questions before this final step, you have been setting a powerful intention for your life as a gift of your own healing and for the people you care about. There is no intention more powerful.

This final step is what serves notice on the physical world of your intention in language that it understands. When you declare your B.I.G. it wakes up all the creative forces of nature to go to work for its fulfillment. You are the word you have spoken, because everything that you are is included in that word. This is far different from keeping a promise you made to someone.

With that said, you may find yourself starting off small or sometimes so big that in both cases you lose steam. If your B.I.G. is large but not impossible you will identify with it as an ambition that over time becomes normalized. If it is too small you will be bored and procrastinate.

Remember it must be thrilling—exciting, inspiring and scary at the same time. So set it on a level where the excitement and the fear it triggers are the same level.

Here are some questions that you may consider as you

- What will I do specifically to share my gift with others?
- By when will I do this?
- Who will my gift impact and in what numbers?

MY BIG IMPOSSIBLE GOAL IS....

____

____

____

____

____

EMBODYING YOUR B.I.G.

So let's pause and take a moment to fill ourselves with gratitude as you reflect on your Finding Your B.I.G. journey.

The following quote by Martha Graham has always helped me to remember that the channel of the Finding Your B.I.G. Journey is within.

"There is a vitality, a life force, an energy, a quickening that is translated through you into action, and because there is

only one of you in all of time, this expression is unique. And if you block it, it will never exist through any other medium and it will be lost. The world will not have it. It is not your business to determine how good it is, nor how valuable, nor how it compares with other expressions. It is your business to keep it yours clearly and directly, to keep the channel open. You do not even have to believe in yourself or your work. You have to keep yourself open and aware to the urges that motivate you. Keep the channel open."
~ ***Martha Graham**, Renowned Choreographer*

How do we keep the channel open?

THE EMBODYING YOUR B.I.G. EXERCISE

Let's take a moment to reflect on what you have accomplished.

Set aside 10 minutes to do this exercise. Have your journal and pen handy to make notes at the end of the exercise.

First let's take a moment to be present to our existence as Spiritual brings, having a human experience. As such we each carry a special, unique and precious gift to be delivered and exchanged with others who are also on this journey.

BREATHE:
Let's take five breaths together to clear our minds and ground ourselves. Together let's breathe in for four counts,

hold our breath for two, and release our breath for six counts.

Do this now.

As you reflect on each step of the journey, remember to stay connected to your breath.

This is our time to REFLECT WITH GRATITUDE, to remind ourselves about why we are here, the times we come alive, who we are, the role we play and the gift we carry.

STEP I ~ VISION

Take a moment to recall your complaint.
This may be a complaint born of the trauma of being silenced, feeling helpless/hopeless, invisible, abandoned and unsafe.

This was the first time in your life you can remember that your light was dimmed.

What is the new story you can tell about this time?

What vision of the world you come from has it allowed you to see?

It is a story not given by the world of our experience, but it came as a flash of desire—a glimpse into what life can be, a world where your complaint would have no existence.

This is the world you come from.

This is the world in your vision.

Bring your vision statement to mind...

"I can see a world where.... for everyone....

STEP II ~ PASSION

Take a moment to bring all your passions to mind, the things you do spontaneously that bring you alive—and that give you a sense of freedom and uniqueness.

Visualize yourself fully immersed in the things you love to do most: a game you love to play or storytelling, singing, creating something, connecting with others...

Bring these passions to mind now. These are the things that reveal your natural comments, discipline and style.

STEP III ~ TALENTS

Take a moment to honor all your talents—the things you do, or the qualities you have that you have been acknowledged for, with payment or thanks.

It may be something we do for work, or some quality for which we are admired.

Take a moment now to acknowledge yourself for these talents.

STEP IV ~ GIFT

Take a moment now to acknowledge the gift you have created with all you talents and passions—the healing gifts for people who have the same complaints and traumas as you do.

Let's take a moment to bring these people to mind.

Who are they?

Where are they?

What do they look like?

What is the gift you have for them?

Imagine yourself delivering this gift; see them receiving this gift.

What does it feel like when you give it and when it is received?

STEP V ~ B.I.G.

Bring to mind your Big Impossible Goal.

How many people will be impacted by your gift and in what ways?

Let's take a deep breath here.

See yourself putting your all into it—all your passions, all your talents.

See it as BIG enough to hold everything you are.

See yourself changing as your goal unfolds. Imagine yourself on a thrilling roller coaster ride.

Can you feel the emotion of anticipation, excitement and fear?

Imagine that right now there is a circle of support gathering around you to see to that it gets done.

See the circle at a table having a meal. There are lots of different kinds of food on the table that each person has brought for the meal. Notice how everyone shares in the meal, passing what they brought to others and inviting them to taste the things they are enjoying.

Notice the sensations in your body.

Breathe.

Take five minutes now and in your journal begin to write down or draw out anything else that came to mind as you were doing this exercise.

Simply write. It doesn't even need to make sense.

Just allow your pen to flow over the paper as you fill up the page.

Keep writing, keep drawing—just flow with whatever comes through for five minutes.

Then pause.

Take a few moments away from what you've written.

Get up from your seat and stretch.

Go back and read through.

Make more notes if more thoughts emerge.

Share what you created during his exercise with a friend and invite your friend to take this journey with you.

Make this exercise a regular practice.

THE MANTRAS OF BLOOMING

Finally, allow me to introduce you to five powerful mantras that you can take with you as you journey. I call them the Mantras of BLOOMING.

Each mantra affirms one of the five elements that enrich our lives.

As you have taken the steps of this journey you are becoming clearer about your VISION, PASSIONS, TALENTS, GIFT and B.I.G. The alignment that you have created here is magnetic and powerful. These mantras are designed to fuel this alignment and strengthen their frequency.

I recommend that you use all five together as a daily practice. As you practice them each day simply allow and receive what is attracted to you.

In this way you will expand massively.

Here are the Mantras.

MINERAL MANTRA

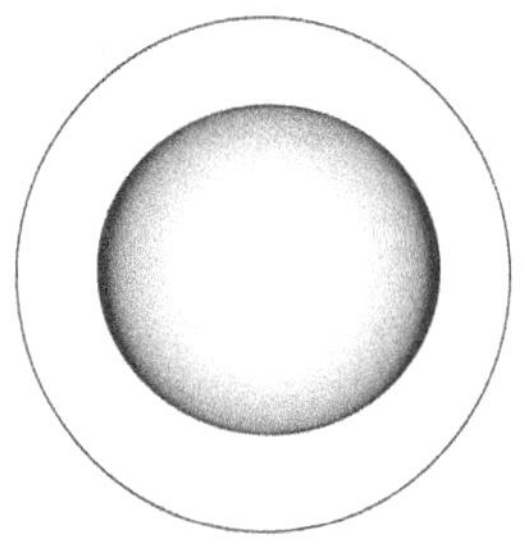

"I can HEAR myself."

NATURE MANTRA

"I can feel myself changing."

FIRE MANTRA

"I can SEE myself."

WATER MANTRA

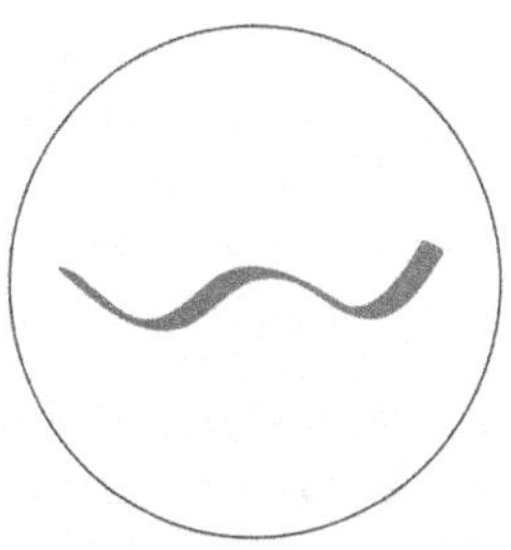

"I am CONNECTED to all life."

EARTH MANTRA

"I am HOME."

To practice these mantras first close your eyes and get still with long slow breaths in and out.

Then with the awareness that "my body is in me" repeat the mantras in the order presented.

Before each of the mantras breathe in deeply. As you breathe all the way silently say the mantras. Breathe fully. all the way in and all the way out. In the space between each mantra pay close attention to all sensations in your body. Do so without judgment. Simply be aware of the sensation.

Notice the insights that come to mind. Catch them and act on them.

The Mantras of BLOOMING can be incorporated into your

morning and evening quiet times or used any time you wish to center yourself and reflect.

Do as many cycles of these mantras as you need.

This is your time to BLOOM!

NEXT STEPS

Thank you for taking this journey. I know that pausing before you move forward required courage. I appreciate you for taking your valuable time to do so. Every insight you have had on this journey adds to a growing body of new knowledge and experience that we at BLOOM would love to hear about.

By taking this journey you have become a member of a global community of BLOOMERS who are eager to meet you and hear your story. We now have a shared language; imagine what we can accomplish together.

For additional support for your journey, please visit www.bloomeducation.institute. There you will also find links to check in as a member of BLOOM. When you check in as a member you will receive a weekly message intended to inspire and celebrate your journey. You will be invited to connect to others who are on a similar journey. You will also be given access to a virtual platform to share your B.I.G.

and create collaborations with other BLOOMERS. Meet-ups, events and destination travel are also in the offering, so stay tuned!

ABOUT THE AUTHOR

Olubode Shawn Brown is the author of **BLOOM, The Essential Journey** ~ *A New Guide to Balance, Growth & Wellbeing*. He is also the founder of **BLOOM Education,** where he helps visionary and creative leaders who are working collectively to negotiate the challenge of working with others, while maintaining a sense of play, sufficiency, balance and wellbeing.

As a child growing up in Jamaica, art was Olubode's first love and passion, but being an artist was not a clear option. In order to be accepted he eventually choose to be a lawyer.

Today, he is the founder of **BLOOM**, a global community of visionaries and creatives from around the world who learn, create and celebrate collectively.

"As a young man coming of age in NYC during the 1980s, I became stuck in a profession I did not love and a religion that offered no refuge at the time, so I embarked on a long journey to reclaim my true voice."

Along the way Olubode has studied with many teachers including **Malidoma Some,** who introduced him to African indigenous spirituality in a way that allowed him to understand it as a cornerstone of his journey to find a home. For over 30 years he has immersed himself in transformational programs, metaphysics, Far Eastern worldviews, and the Christian faith of his childhood to discover what he calls the "Language of BLOOMING."

Olubode's mission is to create media, learning experiences, and events that inform, inspire and celebrate all our human journeys.

ACKNOWLEDGEMENTS

I am grateful to the collective of BLOOMERS around the world who have taken this work into their lives. You have been my teachers. Specifically, I would like to express my gratitude to my brother and friend **Sekou Luke** for seeing the big picture and holding me to it. It was his insistence and caring that produced the ***Finding Your B.I.G. ~ Master Class***. To my bother **Kweku Aacht,** my gratitude for your kind feedback and partnership. Thank you for sharing this work with members of the **AWO Hub** in Accra and using it to build a beautiful community that I can call home. I am grateful to **Chantal Georges**, for receiving, mothering and guiding this work with her gentle presence. **MarQuerite Hamden-Gandy,** thank you for your generosity and holding space for me over many years as these ideas unfolded.

www.ingramcontent.com/pod-product-compliance
Lightning Source LLC
LaVergne TN
LVHW010938110826
845149LV00013B/2655